Pupil Book

2

Series editor   Peter Clarke
Consultant   Len Frobisher
Writing team   Janine Blinko
                    Paula Coombes
                    Hilary Koll
                    Steve Mills
                    Jeanette Mumford

Heinemann is an imprint of Pearson Education Limited,
a company incorporated in England and Wales, having
its registered office at Edinburgh Gate, Harlow, Essex,
CM20 2JE. Registered company number: 872828

Heinemann is a registered trademark of Pearson Education Limited

First published 2002

10 09
10, 9, 8, 7, 6,

ISBN 978 0 435 20554 6

Illustrated by Andy Hammond
Cover illustration by Dave Cockburn
Cover Design by Paul Goodman
Designed by bigtop, Bicester, UK
Printed in China (CTPS/06)

Contents

Let's practise

1 Count and record these things in your classroom.

a windows   **b** doors   **c** chairs   **d** fingers

Let's play   An activity for 2

You need: counters, a container.

185   111   122   144   101

165   134   231   125   221

- Choose one of these numbers each.
- Write your number on a piece of paper and hide it.
- Count out that number of counters.
- Group them so they are easy to count.
- Now swap your counters with your partner.
- Find out your partner's number, by counting their objects.
- Repeat the activity, choosing a different number.

Let's practise

1 Write the numbers that are 10 more and 100 more.

- **a** 11
- **b** 124
- **c** 352
- **d** 532
- **e** 116
- **f** 428
- **g** 93
- **h** 984
- **i** 99

2 Write the numbers that are 10 less and 100 less.

- **a** 124
- **b** 338
- **c** 693
- **d** 387
- **e** 110
- **f** 852
- **g** 963
- **h** 741
- **i** 951

Let's play A game for 2

You need: a set of place value cards for Hundreds, Tens and Units, a paper clip, a labelled paper square and a pencil.

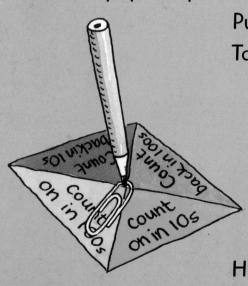

Put the cards face down in 3 piles: H, T, U.

Take turns to:

- Take 3 cards. Make a 3-digit number.
- Spin the paper clip on the spinner.
- Count on or back from your number following the instructions on the spinner.
- Stop when you go past 1000, or 0.
- Write your sequence.

Have 6 turns each.

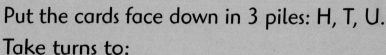

Let's practise

1 Count on in 10s for 10 numbers. Write the numbers.
For example: Start at 48. Write: 58, 68, 78...

a Start at 23   **b** Start at 162   **c** Start at 468

2 Count back in 10s for 10 numbers. Write the numbers.

a Start at 723   **b** Start at 162   **c** Start at 468

Let's play   A game for 2

You need: 24 blank cards, paper and pencil.

Making the game

- Write a sequence of numbers that goes up in 10s.
  You need 8 numbers. Example: 35, 45, 55, 65, 75, 85, 95, 105.

- Write 3 more sequences with
  different starting numbers.

- Write each number on a card.

Playing the game

- Shuffle the cards and place them
  face down in a pile.

- Take turns to take the top card.

- Try to collect a sequence.

- If you need a card, keep it.
  If you don't, put it back at
  the bottom of the pile.

- The first player with a sequence
  of 8 numbers wins!

Let's practise

1 Continue the sequence.

a 1, 3, 5, 7, ___ , ___ , ___ , ___

b 2, 4, 6, 8, ___ , ___ , ___ , ___

c 21, 23, 25, 27, ___ , ___ , ___ , ___

d 95, 97, 99, 101, ___ , ___ , ___

e 64, 62, 60, 58, ___ , ___ , ___ , ___

f 96, 94, 92, 90, ___ , ___ , ___

Let's play **A game for 2**

You need: cards for numbers 51–100.
- Shuffle the cards.
- Place the cards face down in a pile.
- Take turns to take the top 2 cards.
- Try to collect a sequence of odd numbers.
- You need 5 numbers, e.g. 77 79 81 83 85.
- If you need a card, keep it. If you don't, put it back at the bottom of the pile.
- The first player with a sequence of 5 odd numbers wins!

Let's investigate

2 Are these odd or even? How can you tell?

a 243   **b** 244   **c** 531

Let's practise

1 Look at the numbers below.
Write all the numbers that are **between** 250 and 400 **and** even.

322 590 150 329 331 426 287 147 838

413 511 368 288 224 625 263 543 417 251

Let's solve problems

2
- Write any 2-digit number.
- Choose 6 of these rules.

Rules

Count on in 2s	Count back in 2s
Count on in 5s	Count back in 5s
Count on in 4s	Count back in 4s
Count on in 3s	Count back in 3s
Count on in 10s	Count back in 10s
Count on in 100s	Count back in 100s

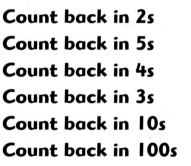

- Write a sequence of 10 numbers for each rule. Start with your 2-digit number each time.

Example: choose 38 and count on in 5s:
38, 43, 48, 53, 58, 63, 68, 73, 78, 83.

- Invent a new rule. Make your own sequence.

Let's investigate

You need: a pile of interlocking cubes.

1 Make these shapes with your cubes.
Make 4 more shapes that grow in the same way.
Write the number of cubes in each shape.
What would the next number be?

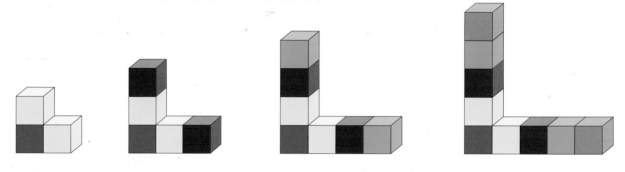

2 Make the next 4 shapes in this pattern.
Write the number of cubes in each shape.
What would the next number be?

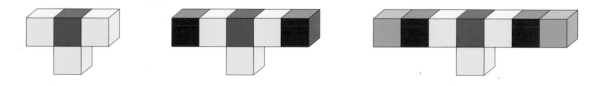

3 Do the same for these shapes.

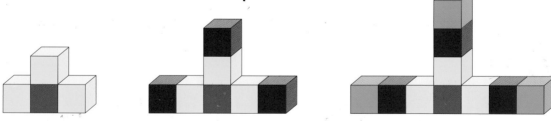

4 Now make your own shape.
Add to it 4 times to see how it grows.
Write the number of cubes in each shape.
What would the next number be?

Let's practise

1 Copy and complete.

a

10 less		10 more
18	28	38
	36	
	295	
	184	
	222	
	306	

b

100 less		100 more
	158	
	264	
	352	
	600	
	901	
	111	

Let's solve problems

2 You need: base-10 apparatus.

- Choose one of the numbers below.
- Make it using base-10 apparatus.
- Record your number.
- Now take another 10-rod.
- Record your new number.
- Keep taking 10-rods until you have written 8 numbers.
- Exchange 10 of the 10-rods for a 100-block if you need to.

- Repeat for 5 other numbers.
- Use the same numbers. Add 100 each time instead of 10.

Let's investigate

1 You need: a blank 0–30 number line, 2 different coloured pencils.

- Start the number line at 0.
- Write all the multiples of 5 in one colour.
- Write all the multiples of 2 in the other colour.
- Which numbers have you written in both colours?

2 Write all the numbers that are multiples of **both** 2 **and** 5.

18   810   25   120
23
105   108   92   150   32
65   253   21   112

Let's practise

1 Look at each number line. Write the multiple of 100.

a
| 94 | 95 | 96 | 97 | 98 | 99 | 100 | 101 | 102 | 103 | 104 | 105 |

b
| 199 | 200 | 201 | 202 | 203 | 204 | 205 | 206 | 207 | 208 | 209 | 210 |

c
| 391 | 392 | 393 | 394 | 395 | 396 | 397 | 398 | 399 | 400 | 401 | 402 |

d
| 793 | 794 | 795 | 796 | 797 | 798 | 799 | 800 | 801 | 802 | 803 | 804 |

e
| 595 | 596 | 597 | 598 | 599 | 600 | 601 | 602 | 603 | 604 | 605 | 606 |

f
| 600 | 601 | 602 | 603 | 604 | 605 | 606 | 607 | 608 | 609 | 610 | 611 |

Let's play   A game for 2

You need: a set of place value cards.

Take turns to:

● Make a 3-digit number with the cards.

● Ask your partner to make the number that is 100 more or 100 less than yours.

5 3 1 ← 6 3 1 → 7 3 1

Record your numbers in a table like this one:

100 less	Starting number	100 more
531	631	731

Let's practise

1 Write these numbers in figures.

six hundred and seventeen   617

a nine hundred and twenty-two

b two hundred and eleven

c six hundred and twenty

d five hundred and forty-three

e four hundred and seven

f three hundred and eighty

2 Write these numbers in words.

474 four hundred and seventy-four

a 774   **b** 375   **c** 453

d 754   **e** 455   **f** 473

g 374   **h** 773

Now use the key to find a 3-letter word for each number you have written.

Example:

four hundred and seventy-four
B   A   T

Use the spellings in the box below.

Key	
seven hundred	S
four hundred	B
three hundred	M
seventy	A
fifty	I
five	N
four	T
three	G
two	D

3 Use the key to make some other words.
Write each 3-letter word as a number in words, and in figures as well.

Let's practise

1 Write the value of the red digit in each number.

a 253   **b** 315   **c** 761   **d** 542   **e** 659

f 908   **g** 189   **h** 420   **i** 837   **j** 497

2 **a** Write all numbers between 300 and 400 containing the digit 6.

    b Now write your numbers in order, starting with the smallest.

Let's investigate

3 The digits 7, 3 and 8 have fallen off.

Write 6 different number plates using these digits.

4 Look at the numbers you have made. Which is

   a the largest number   **b** the smallest number

   c between 690 and 780   **d** between 379 and 730?

5 Work with a partner.

You need: a 0–9 dice.

● Take turns to roll the dice 3 times.

● After each roll, write down the number.   4   9   2

● Use your numbers to make as many 3-digit numbers as you can.

     249   294   429   492   924   942

Let's practise

1 Split these numbers.

a 267 = 2   **b** 382 =   **c** 423 =   **d** 641 =

e 835 =   **f** 540 =   **g** 890 =   **h** 705 =

i 259 =   **j** 302 =   **k** 960 =   **l** 437 =

2 Find each total.

a 400 + 30 + 7 =   **b** 500 + 60 + 2 =

c 600 + 40 + 1 =   **d** 300 + 20 + 0 =

e 700 + 0 + 9 =   **f** 800 + 30 + 0 =

Let's play   A game for 2

You each need: a calculator.

- Enter the same 3-digit number on your calculators.

- Player 1 enters a new number with one of the digits changed.

- Player 2 says what to add or subtract to make the new number, then uses the calculator to check.

352 + 400 = 752

Let's investigate

1 Jamie has 20 red and 20 blue footballs.
He makes a colour pattern, like this.

first   second   third   fourth

He continues the pattern. What colour is the

a seventh football   **b** thirteenth football

c eighteenth football   **d** 21st football

e 33rd football   **f** 38th football?

2 Write True or False.

a The fourth is a Saturday.

b The fifteenth is a Wednesday.

c The eighteenth is a Monday.

d The 22nd is a Tuesday.

e The 27th is two days after the 29th.

f The 21st is a Tuesday.

M	T	W	Th	F	Sa	Su
		1	2	3	4	5
6	7	8	9	10	11	12
13	14	15	16	17	18	19
20	21	22	23	24	25	26
27	28	29	30	31		

Fido's birthday

3 **a** Write all the Thursdays in this
month, like this.   2nd, ..., ..., ...,

b Write all the Wednesdays in this month.

4 Make up some true and false statements
of your own, using the calendar.

Let's practise

1 Which numbers on the plates make the number in the cake?

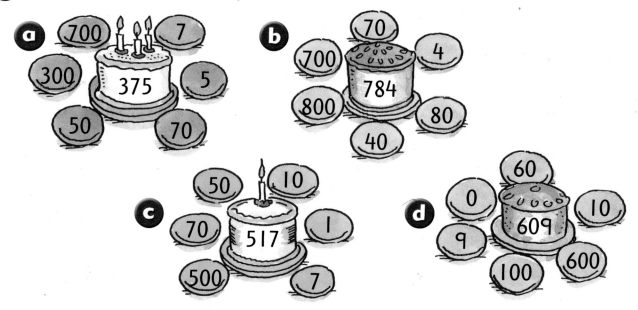

2 Write the cake numbers in order, starting with the smallest.
Leave gaps between the numbers.

3 Now choose a number to write in each gap.
It must lie between the numbers already written.

Let's play A game for 2

You need: a dice.

- Take turns to roll the dice 3 times.
- The first roll is your 100s digit,
  the second roll is your 10s digit
  and the third roll is the units.
- Each say your number.
- The larger number scores a point.
- Score an extra point if you can say a number
  that lies between yours and your partner's.

first   second   third

Let's practise

1 Estimate the number each arrow points to.

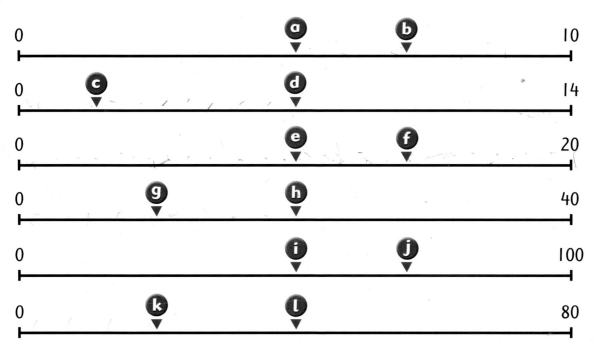

Let's investigate

2 Work with a partner.

You need: a sheet of dotty paper each.

- Tear your dotty paper into 6 different-sized pieces.
- Estimate the number of dots on each one.
- Write your estimate on the back.
- Swap your pieces with your partner.
- Estimate the number of dots.
  Write your estimate on the back.
- Count the dots on each piece.
  Who was closer?

Let's practise

1 Write the numbers that are

    a nearer to 200 than 300   **b** nearer to 500 than 400

    c nearer to 500 than 600   **d** nearer to 800 than 700.

2 Round each number to the nearest 100.

    a 261   **b** 342   **c** 418   **d** 569   **e** 617

    f 577   **g** 683   **h** 936   **i** 842   **j** 915

Let's play   A game for 2

You need: a set of digit cards for numbers 0 to 9.

- Write these numbers in a list.

    100   200   300   400   500   600   700   800   900   1000

- Pick three cards.
  Make a number with   4   8   7
  them, like this.

- Round the number to the nearest 100.   487 ▶ 500

- Cross this number off your list.   500

- Who crosses off all their numbers first?

Let's practise

 Is each set divided into an equal number of objects? YES or NO.

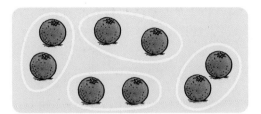

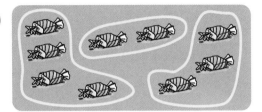

② What fraction of each set of apples is ringed?

3 **ⓐ** What is $\frac{1}{2}$ of 10 pizzas?   **ⓑ** What is $\frac{1}{4}$ of 16 biscuits?

ⓒ What is $\frac{1}{3}$ of 9 cherries?   **ⓓ** What is $\frac{1}{5}$ of 20 buns?

ⓔ What is $\frac{1}{10}$ of 30 peanuts?   **ⓕ** What is $\frac{3}{4}$ of 8 apples?

Let's investigate

4 **ⓐ** This is half a rectangle.
How many squares in the whole rectangle?

ⓑ This is a quarter of a rectangle.
How many squares in the whole rectangle?

Let's practise

1 Use halves, thirds, quarters, fifths and tenths.
Estimate the fraction that is green.
Estimate the fraction that is yellow.

a **b** **c** **d**

e **f** **g** **h**

2 What fraction of each set of hats is ringed?
What fraction of each set of hats is not ringed?

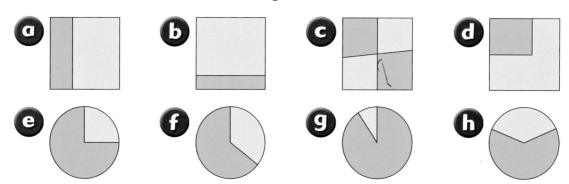

a **b** **c**

Let's solve problems

3 Write a sentence to answer these problems.

a Jamil has 20 conkers to share out at his party but he keeps $\frac{3}{10}$ of them. How many conkers does he keep?

b Amy had 12 cheesy biscuits. She ate $\frac{1}{4}$ of them at the party and took $\frac{3}{4}$ of them to school the next day. How many biscuits did she take to school?

c At Jo's party, the pizza was divided into 10 equal pieces. Jo ate 2 pieces. What fraction of the pizza did she eat?

Let's practise

1 Use the shapes to write a fraction that is the same size.

$\frac{1}{2} =$

$\frac{1}{2} -$

$1 -$

$\frac{1}{5} =$

 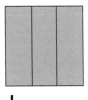

$1 =$

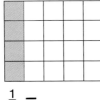

$\frac{1}{5} =$

$\frac{1}{4} =$

$\frac{1}{2} =$

Let's investigate

2 Here are lots of fractions of a cake.

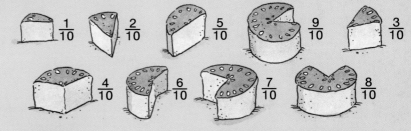

These 2 fractions make a whole cake.

a Write 2 fractions that make a whole cake.
   Do this again with 2 different pieces.

b Write 3 fractions that make a whole cake.
   Do this again with 3 different pieces.

c Write 2 fractions that make half a cake.
   Do this again with 2 different pieces.

Let's practise

1

| 0 | | $\frac{1}{4}$ | | $\frac{1}{2}$ | | $\frac{3}{4}$ | | 1 |

| one quarter |
| half zero |
| three quarters |

Copy and complete.

a One half is larger than _____ quarter.

b Three quarters is larger than one _____ .

c One _____ is between one quarter and three quarters.

d One quarter is smaller than _____ .

Let's solve problems

2 Copy and complete.

  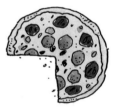

Jo's slice   Anna's slice   Jamil's slice

a Jo's slice is about ____1____ _quater_ of a pizza.

b Anna's slice is about ____a____ _half_ of a pizza.

c Jamil's slice is about _____ _____ of a pizza.

3 Jasmin and Laura ate nearly $\frac{2}{3}$ of a cherry pie between them. Draw their slices and what was left of the pie.

4 Jo's mum made 13 little cakes. The magician made about half of them disappear. How many could be left?

5 Look at the fraction line at the top of the page. Where would you put $\frac{1}{3}$ and $\frac{2}{3}$ on it? Between...

Let's practise

1
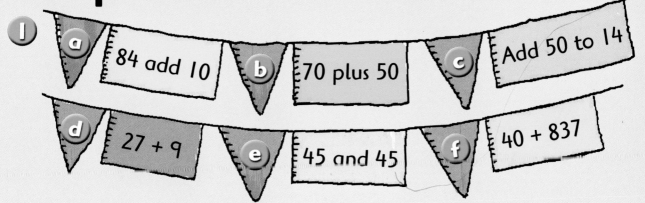

a 84 add 10
b 70 plus 50
c Add 50 to 14
d 27 + 9
e 45 and 45
f 40 + 837

Let's investigate

2 Each party hat has gone up in price.
  Find the new price for each.   11p + 26p = 37p

a

Was 11p. Now 26p more.

b

Was 26p. Now 11p more.

c

Was 42p. Now 31p more.

d

Was 31p. Now 42p more.

e

Was 35p. Now 65p more.

f

Was 65p. Now 35p more.

3 What do you notice about your answers to question 2?

4 You have £2·00. Find all the different pairs of hats you
  could buy at their new price.

Let's practise

① Write the totals of these numbers.

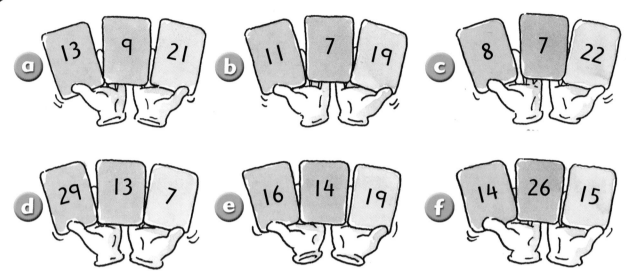

Check your answers by adding in a different order.

Let's investigate

②

Find 4 different cakes with a total of 36.

③ How many different ways can you find of choosing 4 buns with a total of 39?

④ Match the question and answer cards from Activity Sheet 22.

Let's practise

1 Sort these numbers into 2 sets.

387	385	400	270	480
570	290	900	237	600
530	513	124	300	306

multiples of 100	not multiples of 100

2 The numbers on the paper chains have a total of 1000. Write the missing numbers.

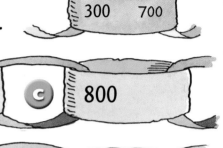

300   700

a 400   b 100   c 800

d 500   e 600   f 700

Let's solve problems

3 There are 1000 people at a party.

a If 300 of them are children, how many are adults?

b If 500 of them are female, how many are male?

Let's play   A game for 2

You will need: cards marked:
100, 200, 300, 400, 500, 600, 700, 800, 900.

● Spread out the cards, face down.

● Take turns to pick 2 cards. Add them together.

● If they total 1000 keep the cards.
  If not, put them back, face down on the table.

● The winner is the player with more cards at the end.

Let's practise

1 These numbers can be split into '5 and a bit'.

$$6 = 5 + 1 \qquad 7 = 5 + 2 \qquad 8 = 5 + 3 \qquad 9 = 5 + 4$$

Use this example to help you add the numbers.

$$15 + 7 \longrightarrow 15 + 5 + 2 = 22$$

a $25 + 9 =$ **b** $35 + 8 =$ **c** $45 + 6 =$

d $55 + 7 =$ **e** $95 + 9 =$ **f** $75 + 8 =$

Let's investigate

2 Find all the different answers you can make by adding any 2 of these numbers.

17	35	26
29	15	18

Split the numbers into 5 and a bit to help you.

3 These are the coins in Rumi's purse.
Which of these items could she pay for exactly?

Let's practise

1 Add these numbers

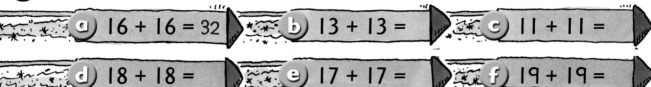

a 16 + 16 = 32 **b** 13 + 13 = **c** 11 + 11 =

d 18 + 18 = **e** 17 + 17 = **f** 19 + 19 =

Let's investigate

2 Choose a number in the grid.
Double your number and add 1.
Double your number and take away 1.
Write your answers like this.

20	17	18
12	15	14
16	19	13

Double 17 = 34.

33   35

Do this for all
the numbers in
the grid.

3 Use your answers to solve these questions.

a 16 + 16 = 32 **b** 13 + 13 =

c 19 + 19 = **d** 19 + 18 =

e 13 + 14 = **f** 16 + 15 =

g 170 + 160 = **h** 120 + 130 =

i 160 + 150 = **j** 130 + 140 =

4 Fiona has 1 more sparkler than her sister.
The total of their sparklers is 45.
How many sparklers does Fiona have?

Clue: What if we had the
same number of sparklers?

Let's practise

1

a 136 + 9 =

b 318 + 11 =

c 283 + 9 =

d 521 + 9 =

e 352 + 11 =

f 927 – 9 =

g 283 – 11 =

h 265 – 9 =

i 378 – 11 =

Let's investigate

2 Choose a number from each box to make a question.

65 + 29 is the same as 65 + 30 – 1 = 94

How many answers can you make?

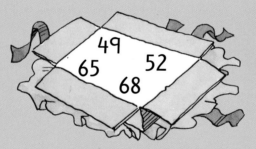

49
65   52
68

+29   +31
–39   –41

3 Choose two darts.

Add the numbers or find the difference between them.

Can you hit all the targets? 39 + 56 = 95

29   47   39   56   41

a 95   **b** 88   **c** 18   **d** 27   **e** 12

Let's practise

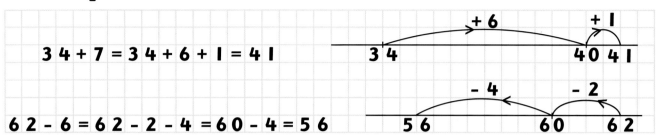

$3\,4 + 7 = 3\,4 + 6 + 1 = 4\,1$

$6\,2 - 6 = 6\,2 - 2 - 4 = 6\,0 - 4 = 5\,6$

1 Answer these questions in your head.

a 58 + 7 =   **b** 75 + 8 =   **c** 84 + 9 =

d 66 + 8 =   **e** 53 + 8 =   **f** 75 + 7 =

g 53 – 7 =   **h** 75 – 8 =   **i** 84 – 9 =

Let's solve problems

2 My mum is 7 years younger than my dad. My dad is 44. How old is my mum?

3 My dad is 9 years older than my mum. My mum is 26. How old is my dad?

4 The difference between my dad's age and my mum's age is 8 years. My dad is 34. How old could my mum be?

5 The difference between my dad's age and my mum's age is 7 years. My mum is 35. How old could my dad be?

6 Pick a number from the pile and add or subtract 7 or 8. How many different ways can you make a number ending in a 3?

Let's practise

Jack, Molly and Ali are adding. They all use a different method.

Jack

467 + 528

400 + 500

60 + 20

7 + 8

900 + 80 + 15 = 995

Molly

467 + 528

528 + 400 = 928

928 + 60 = 988

988 + 7 = 995

Ali

467 + 528

$$\begin{array}{r} 4\ 6\ 7 \\ +\ 5\ 2\ 8 \\ \hline 9\ 0\ 0 \\ 8\ 0 \\ 1\ 5 \\ \hline 9\ 9\ 5 \end{array}$$

① Using one of these methods, or your own method, answer these.

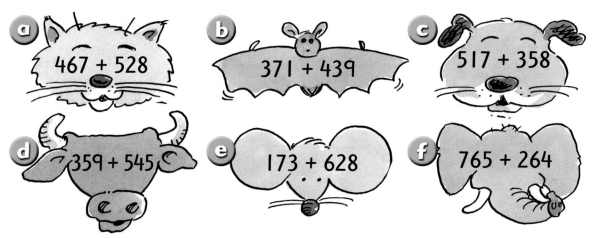

a 467 + 528

b 371 + 439

c 517 + 358

d 359 + 545

e 173 + 628

f 765 + 264

Use a different method to check your answers.

Let's investigate

② You need: digit cards for numbers 0 to 9.

5 8 2 + 1 4 6

Choose 6 cards to make an addition sum like the one above:
Write the answer to the sum. Do this 5 times.
Which of your questions has an answer nearest to 500?

③ If all 6 digits were the same, what could the answer be?

Let's practise

1) Copy and complete these sums to make them correct.

(a)
```
    4 6 7
  +   2 8
    4 0 0
      8 0
      1 5
  _____
    4 ▓ ▓
```

(b)
```
    3 6 4
  +   1 7
    3 0 0
      ▓ ▓
      ▓ ▓
  _____
    3 8 1
```

(c)
```
    5 2 8
  +   6 5
    5 0 0
      8 0
      ▓ ▓
  _____
    ▓ ▓ ▓
```

(d)
```
    7 4 9
  +   5 7
    7 0 0
      ▓ ▓
      ▓ ▓
  _____
    8 ▓ ▓
```

(e)
```
    5 7 5
  +   4 2
    5 0 0
    1 1 ▓
  _____
    ▓ ▓ ▓
```

(f)
```
    6 5 5
  +   5 3
    6 ▓ ▓
    1 0 ▓
  _____
    ▓ 0 ▓
```

(g)
```
    3 4 5
  +   7 5
    ▓ ▓ ▓
    ▓ ▓ ▓
  _____
    ▓ ▓ ▓
```

(h)
```
    8 5 3
  +   5 8
    8 ▓ 0
      ▓ 0
  _____
    ▓ ▓ ▓
```

Let's solve problems

2) Choose two purses. Add the amounts of money.
Which two purses would you need to buy each present?

136p   49p   75p   148p

(a) 211p   (b) 223p   (c) 185p   (d) 197p

Let's practise

1 Write the totals.

a 16 + 3 =   **b** 4 + 14 =   **c** 5 + 14 =

d 7 + 13 =   **e** 12 + 7 =   **f** 6 + 11 =

Use your answers to help with these.

g 19 – 3 =   **h** 18 – 14 =   **i** 19 – 14 =

j 20 – 13 =   **k** 19 – 7 =   **l** 17 – 11 =

2 Copy and complete the questions.

a 8 + ◯ = 17

b 17 – ◯ = 8

c 18 – ◯ = 5

d 5 + ◯ = 18

e 15 – ◯ = 3

f 19 – ◯ = 8

Let's investigate

3 Make up one addition fact and one subtraction fact using the **green** ball.

4 Make as many addition and subtraction facts as you can using 3 of these balls.

Let's practise

① Write all numbers from start to finish.

	Start number	Finish number
a	294	306
c	397	408
e	699	710

	Start number	Finish number
b	489	501
d	798	811
f	598	609

② Copy and complete. Count up from the smaller number.

a 503 – 498 =   **b** 704 – 695 =   **c** 407 – 395 =

d 805 – 792 =   **e** 909 – 898 =   **f** 610 – 596 =

Let's play   A game for 2

You need: 20 counters in 2 colours.

● Take turns to pick 2 numbers on the same colour.

● Work out the difference between them.

● Can you see this number in the grid? If you can, place a counter in your colour on it.

● Your partner must check the answer.

● The winner is the player with more counters on the grid.

6	8	7	6
9	4	5	7
8	6	9	3
9	7	8	5

Let's practise

Sam is subtracting 474 – 59 on paper.

```
4 7 4  =  4 0 0 + 7 0 + 4  =  4 0 0 + 6 0 + 1 4
- 5 9  = -        5 0 + 9  = -        5 0 +  9
                                 4 0 0 + 1 0 +  5 = 4 1 5
```

1 Use Sam's method, or one of your own, to answer these.

a

	5	7	2
–		4	8

b

	4	8	5
–		6	7

c

	3	9	4
–		5	6

d

	8	5	4
–		6	4

e

	3	2	8
–		5	6

f

	7	4	2
–		5	7

How could you check your answers?

Let's investigate

2 Pick a card from each board.

392 481
239 547

– 57 – 63
– 36 – 87

	3	9	2
–		5	7
	3	3	5

How many different answers can you make using the cards?

Check			
	3	9	2
–		5	7
	3	3	5
+		5	7
	3	9	2

Check each of your answers by adding the smaller number to your answer. ➝

Let's practise

Ben is subtracting on paper. Here is his method.

```
  4 8 3   =   4 0 0 + 8 0 + 3   =   4 0 0 + 7 0 + 1 3
- 2 5 7   = - 2 0 0 + 5 0 + 7   = - 2 0 0 + 5 0 +   7
                                     2 0 0 + 2 0 +   6   = 2 2 6
```

1 Use Ben's method, or one of your own, to answer these.

   a 474 – 238   **b** 863 – 549   **c** 592 – 265

   d 726 – 381   **e** 661 – 527   **f** 928 – 366

How could you check your answers?

Let's investigate

2 You need these digit cards.

    1   2   4   5   7   8

Arrange them to make two 3-digit numbers. Then subtract the smaller number from the larger number.

    5   8   2   1   4   7

582 – 147 = 435

   a How many different questions and answers can you make?

   b Which of your questions has the largest answer?

   c Which of your questions has an answer nearest to 0?

3 a Chloe had £3·22. She spent £1·15.
     How much has she now?

   b Chloe had £5·43. She spent £3·18.
     How much has she now?

Let's practise

1 Do these in your head.

  a 94 add 12

  b Add 41 to 50

  c Find the sum of 26 and 9

  d Find the total of 15 and 16

  e 15 take away 7

  f Subtract 21 from 65

  g Find the difference between 70 and 15.

Let's solve problems

2 At Megan's birthday her friends are talking about their ages. How old is each person?

3 Write down the ages of your family or friends. Write some more statements about these ages.

Let's practise

1 Write the value of each coin or note.

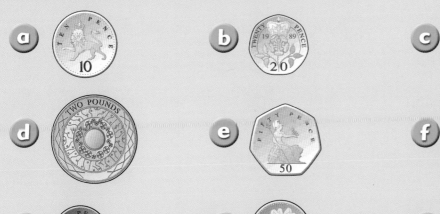

a 10

b 20

c 5

d TWO POUNDS

e 50

f TWO PENCE 2

g ONE PENNY 1

h ONE POUND

i £5 Bank of England FIVE Pounds

2 Write the coins and notes in order, with the smallest value first.

Let's investigate

You need: cards from Activity Sheet 32.

3 Pick a card and find the total of the coins and notes shown. Record your answers like this. 1p + 2p + £1 = £1·03

Continue until you have used all the cards.

4 Find 2 cards that, together, would buy each of these presents with no change.

a £1·63

b £2·03

c £4·46

d £2·52

Let's practise

1 Write a multiplication for each picture.

a How many legs?

b How many legs?

c How many spots?

Let's solve problems

2 Answer these questions.

a Jack reads 10 pages of his book each night. How many pages after 7 nights?

b Molly saves £2 each week. How much after 9 weeks?

c Fiona eats 5 grapes each morning. How many grapes after 10 mornings?

Let's investigate

| = | × | 2 | 5 | 3 | 4 | 10 | 8 |

3 Use these cards to write multiplication questions.

Write each one in two ways, like this. $2 \times 4 = 8$, $4 \times 2 = 8$

Let's practise

1 Copy and complete.

 **a**

$6 \div 2 =$

 **b**

$12 \div 3 =$

c

$9 \div 3 =$

2 Share equally.

 **a**

4   4

$8 \div 2 = 4$

 **b**

$16 \div 2 =$

 **c**

$15 \div 5 =$

3 Write a division for each box.

a 24 cubes divided between 2.
How many each?

$24 \div 2 =$

b 24 cubes divided between 6.
How many each?

c 24 cubes divided between 4.
How many each?

d 24 cubes divided between 8.
How many each?

Let's solve problems

1 There are 13 children at Megan's party.
They all sit at tables.
Write the division with any remainders.

3 children to a table
13 ÷ 3 = 4 r 1

a 2 children to a table   **b** 4 children to a table

c 5 children to a table   **d** 6 children to a table

2 Candles for the cake are 5p each.
How many can each person buy?

a Tom has 19p   **b** Sanjay has 21p

c Emma has 26p   **d** Sam has 29p

Let's play   A game for 2

You need: a set of cards for the numbers 2 to 20.

● Put the cards   **6 to 20**   16   **2 to 5**   3
in 2 piles.   9   12   19   5

● Take turns to pick a card from each pile,   17   4   17 ÷ 4 = 4 r 1
and write a division question.

● Check your answer with your partner.

Let's solve problems

1 Answer these questions about Sandy's party.

a There are 22 children at tables eating birthday cake. The tables hold 4 children. How many tables will Sandy need?

b Sandy gets 19 cards on her birthday. She puts them in piles of 5. How many full piles of 5 are there?

d 28 children are in teams of 3. How many teams of 3 are there?

c Sandy gets £27. She spends it on CDs. Each CD costs £6. How many can she buy?

f 24 toys are put into party bags. Each bag holds 5 toys. How many bags does Sandy need?

e 21 ice creams arrive in boxes. Each box holds 4 ice creams. How many boxes are there?

2 Make up some stories about Sandy's party. Write them as divisions and ask a friend to solve them.

Let's solve problems

1 Write the length of each throw in centimetres.

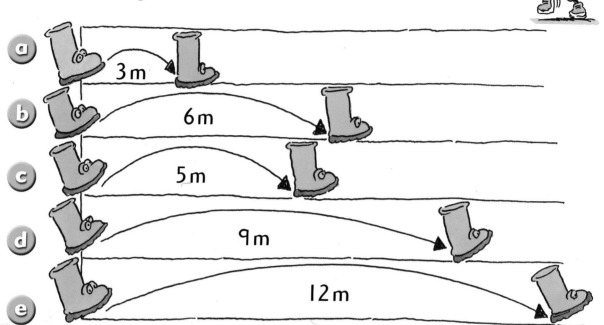

a 3 m

b 6 m

c 5 m

d 9 m

e 12 m

2 There are 10 sweets in each party bag.
How many sweets are there on each table?

a

b

c

d

e

Let's investigate

You need: digit cards for numbers 0 to 9.

3 Pick 2 digit cards to make a 2-digit number.
Multiply the number by 10, and by 100. Write down your
answers. Do this 10 times. What do you notice?

Let's solve problems

1 Answer these questions about Jack's party.

a 29 children came to the party by car. Each car held 4 children.
How many cars were needed?

b A bag holds 25 nuts. How many nuts are in 3 bags?

c Jack says, 'I think of a number. I double it and add 3. The answer is 25.' What is Jack's number?

d There were 37 biscuits on the table. Jack took 6 and Molly took 10.
How many were left?

f There are 18 sweets in the jar and 29 on the table. 25 sweets are eaten.
How many are not eaten?

e 31 packs of crisps were in boxes. Each box held 5 packs of crisps.
How many full boxes were there?

2 Make up some questions of your own about Jack's party.

Let's practise

1 Claire can write a length in 3 ways.
Do the same for these lengths.

2 m   50 cm

250 cm $2\frac{1}{2}$ m

a 1 m 50 cm

b 450 cm

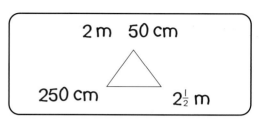

c $8\frac{1}{2}$ m

d 9 m 50 cm

e 750 cm

f $6\frac{1}{2}$ m

Let's investigate

2 Claire made these paper chains.

a 75 cm

b 60 cm

c 85 cm

d 40 cm

If Claire joins any 2 chains she can make 6 different lengths.
Here is one way.

Join a and b.
75cm + 60cm = 135cm
              = 1 m 35 cm

Can you find the other 5 ways?

3 **a** What is the longest paper chain Claire can make with 2 chains?

b Claire joined 3 lengths together. The new chain measured 2 m.
Which paper chains did she choose?

Let's practise

1 Choose the best estimate.

a  3 cm   15 cm   50 cm   **b** 2 cm   25 cm   50 cm

c 5 cm   15 cm   25 cm   **d** ½ m   1 m   3 m

2 Write the best unit for measuring

a the width of a snowflake   **b** the thickness of ice on a pond

c the distance to the ski runs in Scotland.

3 Write the length of each ski run in metres.

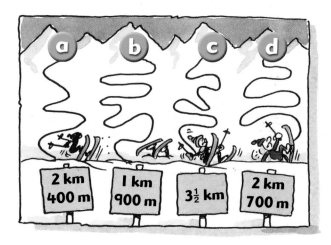

2 km 400 m   1 km 900 m   3½ km   2 km 700 m

4 Make a decoration.

You need: a sheet of A4 paper, scissors.

- Fold the paper in half.
- Draw lines 2 cm apart and about 12 cm long.
- Leave about 1 cm along the left side then the right side as shown in the picture
- Cut along the lines through both layers.
- Pull out carefully.
- About how long is your decoration?

Leave about 1 cm.

Let's solve problems

1 **a** Work out the length of each bear's bed.

Baby	**Mum**	**Dad**
40 cm shorter than Mum's bed	1 m 30 cm	$\frac{1}{2}$ m longer than Mum's bed

b Goldilocks chose the bed that is half the length of Dad's bed. Whose bed did she choose?

2 Dick Whittington and his cat walked 10 km a day. How far did they walk in a week?

3 Widow Twankey's washing line is 5 m long. She needs 2 m 80 cm to hang up Aladdin's shirts. How much line is left?

4 **a** Alice was 1 m 40 cm tall. She drank the shrinking potion. She is now 91 cm tall. How much did she shrink?

b The Queen of Hearts is double Alice's new height. How tall is that?

5 Ali Baba hid in a jar. The jar is 60 cm wide. How many metres long is a line of 5 jars?

60 cm

Let's practise

1 Write each weight to the nearest half-kilogram.

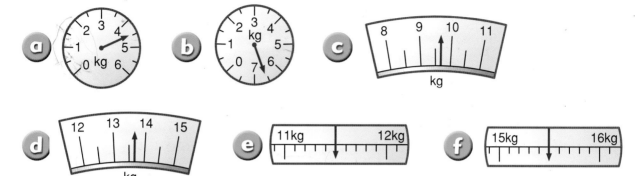

a

b

c

d

e

f

2 Work out the weights of baskets B, C and D.

A

B — $\frac{1}{2}$ kg lighter than A

C — double the weight of B

D — $\frac{1}{2}$ kg heavier than C

3 The farmer has a balance and just 3 weights.
He can put weights in one pan or both pans.

Copy and complete the table
for weighing baskets up to 13 kg.

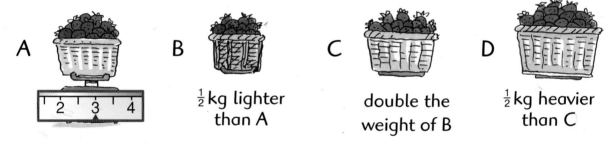

Weight of basket	Left pan	Right pan
1 kg	basket	1 kg
2 kg	basket + 1 kg	3 kg
3 kg		
4 kg		

I can balance baskets of fruit from 1 kg to 13 kg.

Let's solve problems

Apple and blackberry pie	
shortcrust pastry	350 g
sugar	100 g
apples	450 g
blackberries	200 g

Pumpkin pie	
shortcrust pastry	175 g
sugar	25 g
pumpkin	250 g
apples	200 g
currants	100 g

Raspberry pie	
shortcrust pastry	225 g
sugar	50 g
raspberries	700 g

1 Work out the uncooked weight of each pie in grams.

2 Jasmine's mum makes one of each pie.

   a What is the total weight in grams of

- shortcrust pastry
- sugar
- apples?

   b Which pie has the most fruit?

3 Jasmine's mum makes 1 apple and blackberry pie and 2 raspberry pies.

   a What did the pies weigh altogether in kilograms and grams?

   b There was half an apple and blackberry pie left over. About how many grams will it weigh?

Let's practise

1 How much juice is in each jug to the nearest half-litre?

a $1\frac{1}{2}\, l$

b

c

d

e

f

g

h

Let's investigate

2 Juice is added to jugs **a** to **d** to the 5-litre mark
and to jugs **e** to **h** to the 10-litre mark.
How many litres are added to each jug?

3 Bud is mixing paint to decorate his juice bar.
He mixes whole tins of paint each time.
How many litres of these colours will he make?

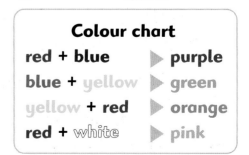

a purple   **b** green   **c** orange   **d** pink

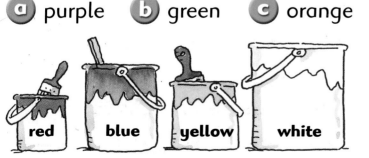

red	blue	yellow	white
2 l 500 ml	10 l	5 l	12 l 500 ml

Colour chart

red + blue	▶	purple
blue + yellow	▶	green
yellow + red	▶	orange
red + white	▶	pink

Let's practise

1 **a** Copy and complete.

1 litre fills 5 cups.

2 litres fill ___ cups.

3 litres fill ___ cups.

4 litres fill ___ cups.

5 litres fill ___ cups.

___ litres fill 50 cups.

b How many millilitres of tea does each cup hold?

Let's solve problems

2 Ice cream is sold in tubs of these sizes.

a  1 litre **b**  2 litres **c**  4 litres **d**  8 litres

How many 100 ml helpings can you get from each tub?

3 Miss Gold needs 20 cones for her class.
Each cone holds 50 ml of ice cream.
Which size of tub should she buy?

4 Meena is helping at the class summer party.

a She fills the jug from the carton.
How much juice is left in the carton?

b She pours out 3 cups of juice.
How much juice is left in the jug?

c How many cups can she fill from
● a full jug   ● a full 2-litre carton?

Let's solve problems

1 Write each time in 2 ways.

   a 1:45   **b** 6:05   **c** 4:25   **d** 10:50

one forty-five
quarter to two

2 Write the digital time to match.

   a half past 12   **b** quarter past 10   **c** 5 past 11

     12:30

   d 10 to 10   **e** 25 past 6   **f** 15 minutes to 4

   g 20 to 9   **h** 5 minutes to 1   **i** quarter to 8

3 Write the digital time 10 minutes later.

   a 2:35   **b** 9:05   **c** 8:50   **d** 7:55

   e 10:15   **f** 6:45   **g** 1:55   **h** 12:20

4 Write the analogue time 10 minutes earlier.

   a 12:35   **b** 9:05   **c** 9:10   **d** 7:55

   e 3:40   **f** 6:45   **g** 5:50   **h** 1:05

Let's practise

1 Copy and complete using the list of numbers.

_____ minutes ▶ I hour		**365**
_____ hours ▶ I day		**60**
_____ days ▶ I week		**7**
_____ months ▶ I year		**24**
_____ weeks ▶ I year		**12**
_____ days ▶ I year		**52**

Let's solve problems

2 Write the unit of time for measuring

a cooking a birthday cake

b blowing out the candles

c watching the magician

d opening a present

e playing a game

f blowing up a balloon.

3 Look at the birthday party scenes in question 2. What takes about

a 10 seconds   **b** I minute   **c** 10 minutes   **d** I hour?

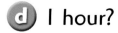

Let's investigate

1 In May, how many days were

  a Mondays **b** Tuesdays

  c Fridays **d** Saturdays?

May						
S	M	T	W	Th	F	Sa
			1	2	3	4
5	6	7	8	9	10	11
12	13	14	15	16	17	18
19	20	21	22	23	24	25
26	27	28	29	30	31	

2 Write the day of the week for

  a 23 May **b** 13 May

  c 3 May **d** 7 May

  e the first day in May

  f the last day of the month

  g a fortnight after 5 May.

Let's solve problems

3 Four friends have their 8th birthday in May.

  a Write the date of each boy's birthday.
  - Joel   first Sunday
  - Max   second Saturday
  - Tom   third Thursday
  - Robbie   last Tuesday

  b How many days older is
  - Joel than Max
  - Max than Tom
  - Tom than Robbie?

  c How many days younger is
  - Tom than Joel
  - Robbie than Max?

Let's practise

1 Copy and complete. Tick the shapes that are prisms.

Shape	a	b	c	d	e	f	g	h	i
Prism	✓	✗							

> The 2 end-faces of a prism are the same shape.

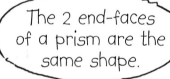

Let's solve problems

2 Which present did each friend bring? Name the shape.

a Nina's present has
6 rectangular faces,
8 vertices,
12 edges.

b Andy's present has
1 curved face,
2 circular faces,
2 curved edges.

c Rupa's present has
2 triangular end-faces,
all other faces are
rectangles.

d Tommy's present has
hexagonal end-faces,
12 vertices,
6 rectangular faces.

Let's practise

1 Sort the shapes.
Make a table. Put a ✓ for yes and a ✗ for no each time.

	Quadrilateral	5 vertices	Sides same length
a	✓	✗	✗
b			

Let's investigate

2 Read the clues. Find the shape and write its name.

a My four sides are different lengths.

quadrilateral

b I am half of a circle.

c I am a symmetrical shape with 6 vertices.

d I am a quadrilateral with 4 right angles.

e I have 5 equal sides.

f I have 1 right angle and fewer than 4 vertices.

3 You need: 12 straws all the same length.

- Without bending the straws, make five squares.
- Draw the shape you make.

Let's investigate

You need: red, yellow, blue and green interlocking cubes.

 Build these shapes.

 a

 b

Make a table like this.
Count the square faces
you can see.

Shape	Number of faces			Total
	Red	Yellow	Blue	
a		5		
b				

2 Use 4 cubes to build these.

 a    b    c    d

Make a table.
Count the faces.

Shape	Number of faces				Total
	Red	Blue	Green	Yellow	
a	5	5	4	4	
b					
c					

3 True or false?

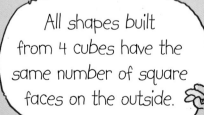

All shapes built
from 4 cubes have the
same number of square
faces on the outside.

Make 2 more
shapes from 4
cubes. Count
the faces on
the outside.

Let's investigate

You need: a mirror, sheets of A4 paper, scissors.

1 Use your mirror to test each shape.
Copy and complete the table.

Lines of symmetry	Shapes
none	
one	a
more than one	

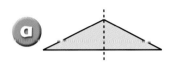

2 Make party decorations.

- Fold a sheet of paper into quarters.
- Draw and cut out a design.
- Draw lines of symmetry on your
cutouts and frames.

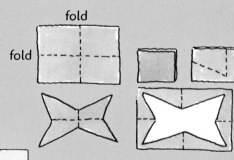

fold

fold

Now make a party chain.

- Cut a strip of paper.
- Fold it to make a zig-zag.
- Fold the zig-zag in half.
- Draw and cut out a design.
- Mark the lines of
symmetry in the chain.

fold

Keep the corners to link your chain.

Let's investigate

You need: a right-angle measurer.

1 Find which slices are right angles.

 a  b c  d e

2 Test these angles for size.
Copy and complete the table.

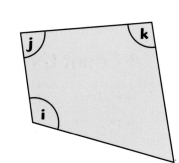

Less than a right angle	About a right angle	Greater than a right angle
a		

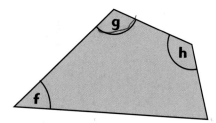

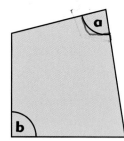

3 Find 2 lolly sticks that are at right angles to each other.

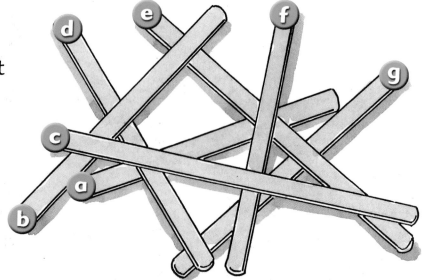

Let's investigate

1 Work with a partner.
You need: ten 1p coins, a yoghurt pot.

- Write the numbers 0 to 10 on a piece of paper.
- Put all the coins in the pot. Cover the top and shake it.
- Tip them out on to the table.
- Count the number of coins showing heads.
- Put a tick next to that number on your piece of paper.
- Do this 10 times.
- Write 3 questions about your chart.

2 Do the activity 10 more times.
Are the answers to your questions still the same?

3 This is the chart that Martin and Gary
made when they tried the activity.

- Compare Martin and Gary's chart with yours.
- Write some sentences about how the charts are the same.
- Write some sentences about how they are different.

Let's practise

1 Write these numbers as tallies.

a 16   **b** 4   **c** 10   **d** 17

e 14   **f** 9   **g** 28   **h** 32

2 Write these tallies as numbers.

a ЍЍ ЍЍ   **b** ЍЍ IIII   **c** ЍЍ ЍЍ ЍЍ IIII

d ЍЍ ЍЍ II   **e** ЍЍ II   **f** ЍЍ ЍЍ ЍЍ ЍЍ ЍЍ I

Let's investigate

3 Work with a partner.

You need: a box of coloured cubes.

● Make a table like this:

Colour of cube	Tally	Total
Red		
Yellow		
Green		
Blue		

● Take turns to pick a cube from the box.

● Keep a tally of what colours the cubes are.

● Use the cubes to build a wall.

● When all the cubes have been used, work out the totals.

4 Look at the completed table.
Write 3 sentences about the cubes.

Let's investigate

Favourite party food for Year 2 children.

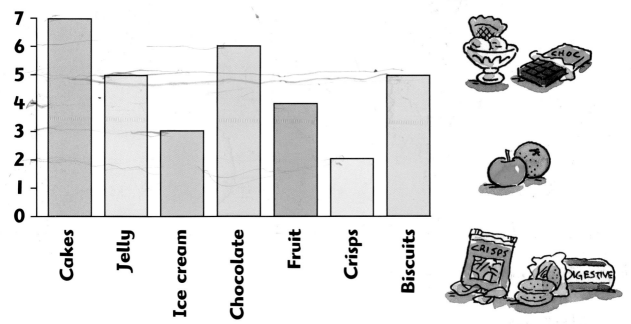

1 Look at the information in the bar chart. Copy and complete the table.

Party food	Tally	Total
Cake		
Jelly		
Ice cream		
Chocolate		
Fruit		
Crisps		
Biscuits		

2 Which of these sentences are true and which are false?

a Cake is the most popular party food.

b The least popular party food was ice cream.

c More children chose jelly than fruit.

d Twenty-six children were asked about their favourite party food.

Let's investigate

1 Children at Trinity School were asked about their favourite pets. This bar chart shows their answers.

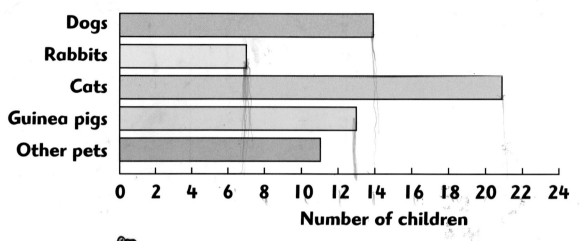

a How many children voted for dogs?

b How many children voted for guinea pigs?

c How many more children voted for cats than rabbits?

d Which animal had fewer than 10 votes?

e Some children voted for other pets. Suggest 3 pets they might have been thinking of.

f Who might find the information in the bar chart useful?

2 Ask the children in your class about their favourite pets. Draw a bar chart like the one in question 1.